M
23.70

MCR

EVANSTON PUBLIC LIBRARY

W9-AMS-984

x523.6 Boekh.P

Boekhoff, P. M. (Patti
Marlene), 1957-
Comets / by P.M.
Boekhoff and Stuart

JAN 3 1 2003

EVANSTON·PUBLIC
LIBRARY

*Purchase of this library
material made possible
by a contribution
to the Fund for Excellence*

Eyes on the Sky

Comets

by P.M. Boekhoff and Stuart A. Kallen

EVANSTON PUBLIC LIBRARY
CHILDREN'S DEPARTMENT
1703 ORRINGTON AVENUE
EVANSTON, ILLINOIS 60201

**KIDHAVEN
PRESS**™

THOMSON
GALE

San Diego • Detroit • New York • San Francisco • Cleveland
New Haven, Conn. • Waterville Maine • London • Munich

© 2003 by KidHaven Press. KidHaven Press is an imprint of The Gale Group, Inc.,
a division of Thomson Learning, Inc.

KidHaven™ and Thomson Learning™ are trademarks used herein under license.

For more information, contact
KidHaven Press
27500 Drake Rd.
Farmington Hills, MI 48331-3535
Or you can visit our Internet site at http://www.gale.com

ALL RIGHTS RESERVED.
No part of this work covered by the copyright hereon may be reproduced or used in any form
or by any means—graphic, electronic, or mechanical, including photocopying, recording, taping,
Web distribution or information storage retrieval systems—without the written permission of
the publisher.

LIBRARY OF CONGRESS CATALOGING-IN-PUBLICATION DATA

Boekhoff, P.M.
  Comets / by P.M. Boekhoff and Stuart A. Kallen.
    p. cm.—(Eyes on the sky)
Includes bibliographical references and index.
Summary: Discusses the discovery of comets, their life, death, and the mysteries
associated with them.
  ISBN 0-7377-0999-5 (hardback : alk. paper)
  1. Comets—Juvenile literature. [1. Comets.] I. Kallen, Stuart A., 1955– II. Title.
III. Series.
  QB721.5 .B64 2003
  523.6—dc21

2001006268

Printed in the United States of America

Table of Contents

1
Discovery of the Comet

When a comet streaks across the sky, it looks like a bright star with a long tail of light behind it. And, in fact, the tail is what defines a comet—without it, a comet would just be a rock streaking through space. The ancient Greeks named comets for the appearance of their tails, which they thought looked like hair. The word *comet* comes from the Greek word *kometes*, which means "long hair."

Comets **orbit** around the sun in a long, oval path. A comet may be as big as a school bus, a football stadium, a giant mountain, or even a small planet. Comets come from far away, loop very close to the sun, then return to deep space before they orbit the sun again. After this journey, a comet will sometimes disappear for many years.

Comets are made out of ice, **gas**, and loose carbon dust that looks like charcoal. The ball of dust, gas, and ice is called the **nucleus**. When a comet is far away from the sun, it looks like a small dark planet invisible from Earth.

The Comet Grows a Tail

As the comet travels closer to the sun, several things happen: The ice warms up and turns into a misty cloud of gas called a coma. This

Artwork depicts a blue-white comet streaking across the sky, a long tail of light trailing behind.

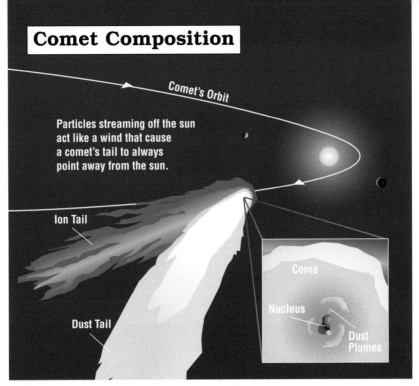

Comet Composition

Comet's Orbit

Particles streaming off the sun act like a wind that cause a comet's tail to always point away from the sun.

Ion Tail

Dust Tail

Coma

Nucleus

Dust Plumes

cloud is large, thick, bright, and about a thousand times bigger than the nucleus. Together, the nucleus and the giant coma form the head of the comet.

When the coma glows in the sunlight, it releases hydrogen, the lightest and most plentiful gas in the universe. The lightweight hydrogen gas escapes from the nucleus and forms a large layer around the coma, called the hydrogen envelope—a very thin invisible cloud made from extremely small droplets of water.

This hydrogen envelope grows very large, millions of miles across. But the actual amount of material in the envelope is very small. If it were pushed together, it would only fill an average suitcase. Though the coma may grow larger than the sun itself, the comet is still not hot enough to make a blaze through the sky.

As it travels closer to the sun, the comet gets fiery hot, causing jets of gas and dust to erupt from the nucleus. The heat of the sun blows the dust and gas back from the nucleus, creating the comet's beautiful glowing tail, which can be seen from Earth as it streams across the sky.

Heavenly Bodies

Comets are objects of great mystery and wonder that have been studied for centuries. Astronomers all over the world recorded the passing of comets, noting the place they appeared in the sky. In the 1600s British scientist Sir Isaac Newton proved that comets traveled in orbits like planets. His friend British astronomer Edmond Halley convinced him to write his ideas down and even paid to have them published.

Halley used Newton's theories to compare the orbits of specific comets that had been seen over the years. He knew that if a comet moved in an orbit, it must return to the same place in the sky at a specific time. In 1682 Halley became the first known person to discover exactly when a comet would return.

Halley noticed that the records of early astronomers showed that the bright comet he saw in 1682 and the bright comets that earlier

Edmond Halley is the first known person to predict when a comet would return to the same place in the sky.

astronomers had seen in 1531 and 1607 had very similar orbits. He came to the conclusion that all three were really the same comet.

Halley believed the comet had made a complete orbit and returned to the same place in the sky, becoming visible about every seventy-six years. Based on this idea, Halley predicted the comet would return in 1758–1759. Although he did not live to see the comet return, when it did, it was named Halley's comet to honor his discovery.

Halley's Comet

Halley's comet returned to light up the sky again in 1835, after seventy-six years as a dark, invisible little planet. Astronomers aimed their telescopes at the sky and made drawings of the comet. Looking at Halley's comet that year, English astronomer John Herschel noticed that the sun was blowing out huge amounts of electricity and light. The hot wind of the sun seemed to blow on comet Halley, affecting the shape of its tail. This powerful force later came to be known as the **solar wind**.

When Halley's comet came back around in 1910, the telescopic camera had been invented, and astronomers took the first pictures of the comet. People gathered on rooftops and hilltops, and astronomers watched from observatories all over the world to get a closer view of the comet. The comet passed very close to the sun that year and became very bright. But it would be

Halley's comet appears in the same place in the sky once every seventy-six years.

another seventy-six years before anyone could get a truly close-up view of Halley's comet.

When it returned in 1986, Halley's comet was viewed by several space probes from different countries sent to gather information about it. The former Soviet Union sent *Vega 1* and *2*, the European Space Agency sent *Giotto*, and two Japanese spaceships watched as the comet passed. Close-up pictures of the comet's nucleus showed that it is made of loose, very dark dust. The nucleus is full of small holes, allowing the gases to mingle with the dust. The outside of the nucleus is darker than coal, making the comet one of the darkest objects in the solar system.

Comet Borrelly

Because of its predictable orbit, Halley's is one of the most studied comets. But other comets have also been the focus of scientific research.

In October 1998 the U.S. space agency NASA launched *Deep Space 1* to test new technologies in space. It was almost out of fuel when it passed close to comet Borrelly on September 22, 2001. The pictures it took of Borrelly's nucleus are the closest, clearest pictures ever taken of a comet.

Comet Borrelly looks like a small planet being formed by fire and ice. Its nucleus is about five miles long and is shaped like a bowling pin. Some parts of the nucleus are smooth and some parts are rough. It looks like an odd-shaped planet, with mountains, volcanoes, and cliffs where the rocky crust has cracked. The whole surface of the nucleus is covered with a darkened crust of sooty rock, and the inside is believed to be mostly ice.

In the middle of the nucleus are smooth rolling plains with bright areas that seem to be the source of dust jets. These jets spout from the plains on the comet, which seem to be wearing away as the dust spews off the surface. There are many jets blowing in different directions, and the largest seems to be split into at least three parts.

NASA's *Deep Space 1* satellite swoops past comet Borrelly. *Deep Space 1* took this photo (inset) on its mission.

At both ends of the nucleus, the land is rough and uneven, with many chains of high mountains creating a jagged line between day and night on the comet. This rough landscape contains very dark patches that appear to be higher than the areas around them. Some of the darkest parts seem to be on top of mountain peaks, where the carbon dust looks to be piled the highest. In some places the dark material makes the grooves and cracks easier to see. The cracks appear to be fractures, caused by the breaking and shifting of a rocky crust.

Comets such as Borrelly have so much in common with other objects in space, they seem to show that all heavenly bodies are related. Astronomers think mysterious comets may hold many wondrous secrets, including how planets—and even human life—were formed.

2
The Life of a Comet

Comets are believed to be some of the oldest objects in the solar system, made out of the first materials formed in our solar system about 4.6 billion years ago. American astronomer Karen Bjorkman thinks that comet clouds are made as a part of any planetary system that forms around a star. She thinks this because she observed comets in deep space falling toward a young star called HD 163296, which is creating its own solar system.

Birth of a Comet

Scientists believe that when our solar system began, the sun first ignited to form the center of the solar system, then blew lighter material, such as dust and gas, out into space. The heavier materials formed the inner planets, including Earth. Eventually the lightest materials were pressed tightly together to form the outer planets: Jupiter, Saturn, Uranus, and Neptune. Far from the sun, these giant gas planets orbit in the cold, dark part of the solar system.

Some of the gas and dust in the area far from the sun did not get pressed together and formed into planets. When the planets and moons gathered material from space into giant balls, the comets remained free and did not combine with other space materials. The comets stayed in orbit in cold places very far from the sun. This is where comets come from when they begin their journey toward the sun.

Cold Storage

In 1950 Dutch astronomer Jan Henrik Oort proposed the idea that comets live in a cold storage cloud far beyond the orbits of the outer planets of the solar system. About 100 billion comets slowly orbit the sun in what has been named the Oort Cloud. Comets that live in the Oort Cloud are called long-period comets because it takes them a long time—more than two hundred years—to travel from the Oort Cloud to the sun and back.

In 1951 American astronomer Gerard Kuiper suggested that some comets come from an area now known as the Kuiper Belt—an area about

A computer simulation shows the Oort Cloud, home to 100 billion orbiting comets.

a billion miles wide just outside the orbit of Neptune. Pluto, the ninth planet from the sun, is the largest object in the Kuiper Belt. Pluto is about one-sixth the size of Earth (more than fourteen hundred miles wide), and some scientists believe it may be one of many truly gigantic comets!

Astronomers believe the belt contains millions of comets, though they have only studied a small part of this mysterious faraway zone. Thousands of these comets are very large, from sixty to two hundred miles across. Looking at this area through the Hubble Space Telescope, astronomers have also seen small cometlike objects a few miles across, about the size of New York's Manhattan Island.

The Kuiper Belt is about a hundred times closer to the sun than the Oort Cloud. The comets that exist there are called short-period comets. It takes them less than two hundred years to orbit once around the sun. This group includes comet Enke. With a period of 3.2 years,

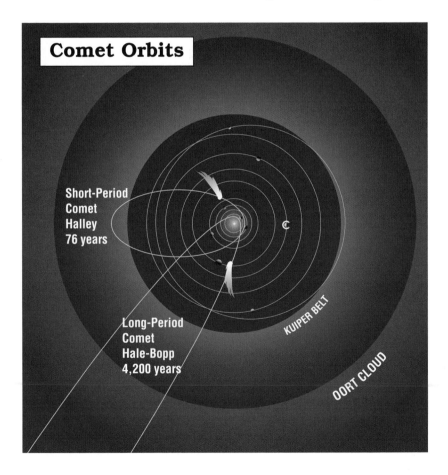

Comet Orbits

Short-Period Comet Halley 76 years

Long-Period Comet Hale-Bopp 4,200 years

KUIPER BELT

OORT CLOUD

Enke circles the sun faster than any other known comet.

Comet Enke is one of the main comets on the Comet Nucleus Tour (CONTOUR), a NASA mission to study comet nuclei in 2003–2008. By studying the nuclei of comets, astronomers can understand how individual comets are alike or different from one another. The CONTOUR spacecraft will observe the comets when they are close to the sun and burning brightly.

Comet Tails

Enke is thought to be a very old comet that has passed by the sun many times. Astronomers believe its ice and gases will soon burn out. As the ice and gases start to fizzle out, the comet's geyser holes will become smothered in space dust. When Enke's geyser holes plug up, it will no longer grow a tail. Such objects without a tail are called asteroids. An asteroid is a small, rocky, planetlike object that orbits around the sun.

The brightest kind of comet tail is the dust tail. It can be more than 200 million miles long, or so short that it is almost invisible. The dust tail is wide and curved and glows white. The dust tail is caused by the pressure of the intense sunlight burning off the largest, heaviest, most solid parts of the comet. Dust tails tend to be curved because the heavier materials fall through the sky as the comet swings around the sun. The thick white dust sometimes glows yellow or red as the different types of carbon, rock dust, iron, and other metals **reflect** sunlight.

Hale-Bopp's Tails

In 1995 NASA's Hubble Telescope took pictures of comet Hale-Bopp showing that the dust tail was shaped like a pinwheel. The nucleus was spinning around in a complete circle about once a week, spraying out a spiraling tail. Along the spiral, a bright cloud appeared. The cloud may have been a piece of Hale-Bopp's icy crust that was spun into space.

Like many comets, Hale-Bopp has a second thin, straight, and longer tail, called an **ion** tail or gas tail, which glows blue. The ion tail is made of light, electrically charged **particles** of water and explosive elements that are similar to gasoline and rocket fuel. The solar wind plays with the ion tail, twisting it and making it dance with ever-changing rays and streamers. Sometimes the solar wind plays tricks with Hale-Bopp's tail, making it disappear and reappear in another place.

Astronomers discovered a third type of tail—invisible to the naked eye—on Hale-Bopp. Like the ion tail, it shoots straight out, but it is very

Comet Hale-Bopp, with its gas and dust tails shown, flies over Mono Lake, California.

narrow and points in a slightly different direction. From close up, it has a faint yellow glow, which is caused by sodium atoms. Scientists study the colors in a comet's tails to find out what kinds of elements are being burned off by the sun.

Comet Hyakutake

The bright comet Hyakutake lit up the sky with red, yellow, green, blue, and purple for more than two months in 1996. The beautiful, brilliant colors mean that a lot of ice, gas, rock, and metal are burning off, which can cause a comet to break apart.

Pictures taken of comet Hyakutake on March 25, 1996, by the Hubble Space Telescope showed that most of the dust in the tail was created on the side of the nucleus facing the sun. As the nucleus spun around in the sunlight, the icy parts shot out large amounts of dust in a faint jet. Sunlight striking the dust turned the jet around and blew it back to the side of the nucleus facing away from the sun.

Chunks of the coarse-grained carbon dust broke off from the nucleus of Hyakutake. The dust balls were too big to speed up and become part of Hyakutake's tail. They became small

Comet Hyakutake, surrounded by dust, as it appeared in a photo taken by the Hubble Space Telescope on March 25, 1996.

comets, forming their own tails. Comets are usually about one to ten miles wide, while small comets are about the size of a house.

When comets start to break apart, they are coming closer to the end of their lives. The sun, which causes them to burn with a glorious light, is tearing them apart. Although comets can go through many changes and many lives, they tend to move in patterns that can be predicted and observed. But each comet is different, and sometimes they act in unexpected ways. Much of what is known about comets comes from studying them as individuals and recording their behavior.

3
The Death of a Comet

Born in the coldest, darkest parts of the solar system, trillions of comets orbit in outer space far from Earth. Only a small number of comets ever leave these frigid regions to make a journey toward the blazing sun. And these comets move closer to the sun's scorching heat than any other heavenly body.

Not every comet hurling through space circles the sun, however. There are many other objects in the universe, such as planets, that may act upon a comet, causing it to plunge to a fiery death. And the random effects of cold, heat, and **gravity** determine the life and death of a comet.

It is gravity that pulls comets toward larger heavenly bodies such as the sun or Jupiter. Some comets are pulled out of cold storage by the gravity of the sun, passing stars, or by planets or other objects traveling through space. When a comet is yanked out of the cold places far from the sun, it travels faster and faster as an object's gravity pulls it in.

The sun is by far the largest object in the solar system. Its gravity pulls hard on everything around it, causing the entire solar system to orbit around it. When a comet is pulled toward the sun, it must pass through the orbits of the giant outer planets. The gravity of the giant outer planets also pulls on the comets.

Jupiter, which is big and hot and fiery—like a mini-sun—pulls especially hard on the comets. Sometimes Jupiter pulls a comet around it for a while, then lets it go so it is flung out of the solar system. There, objects

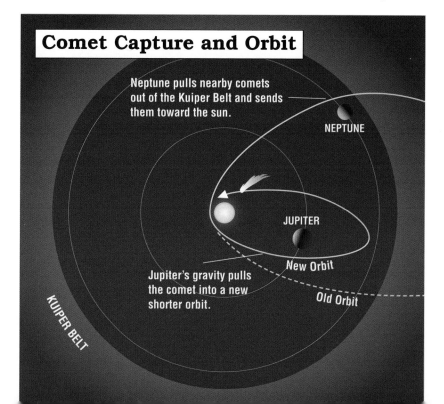

Comet Capture and Orbit

Neptune pulls nearby comets out of the Kuiper Belt and sends them toward the sun.

NEPTUNE

JUPITER

New Orbit

Jupiter's gravity pulls the comet into a new shorter orbit.

Old Orbit

KUIPER BELT

with even more powerful gravity than the sun may pull a comet in.

Comet Groups

More often a close encounter with Jupiter or the other outer planets pushes a comet closer to the sun. If this happens, the comet can plunge to its death as it crashes into the sun or one of the planets. The fiery sun or the **atmosphere** of a warm planet boils the ice away quickly, sometimes causing the comet to explode into pieces.

Comet Shoemaker-Levy, for example, split into twenty-one parts when Jupiter's strong gravity pulled it in. For one week in July 1994, pieces of the comet crashed into Jupiter's at-

An artist's illustration shows comet Shoemaker-Levy colliding with Jupiter.

mosphere, exploding and releasing fireballs bigger than Earth. For months after the crash, a string of large dark scars appeared where pieces of the comet entered Jupiter's atmosphere.

Sometimes a comet also breaks up in this way when it flies too close to the sun. If it does not plunge to a fiery death, its nucleus may split up into parts. This happened to comet West in 1975. Out of one parent comet, a family of four smaller comets was born.

Comet Ikeya-Seki

When a comet—like West—breaks up into pieces, it may form a string of comets that travel in the same orbit, grazing by the sun one by one on their next visit. They are called sungrazers because they pass very close to the sun and brighten very quickly. Most sungrazers are thought to have once been part of a very large parent comet that split up into parts when it passed very close to the sun. The most famous of these is the comet Ikeya-Seki, which travels with a family group of seven comets.

Ikeya-Seki became a brilliant comet when it was seen grazing by the sun in 1965. Ikeya-Seki's nucleus broke open and split into two or three nuclei as it neared the sun, but it did not come apart. The comet survived a close encounter with the sun, becoming so bright, it could be seen in full daylight.

American astronomer Brian G. Marsden has found evidence that Ikeya-Seki and an even more brilliant comet that appeared in 1882 both split away from an even bigger comet that appeared in 1106. This comet and all the others in its comet group may have split away from a truly giant comet thousands of years ago.

Some sungrazers crash into the sun, but those that survive leave a trail of small comets and cosmic comet dust in their paths. As Earth moves in its orbit, it may pass the orbit of a comet. When this happens, the larger pieces of cosmic dust, known as meteors, burn up in the

A NASA spacecraft captures two sungrazers plunging through the solar atmosphere very near to the sun.

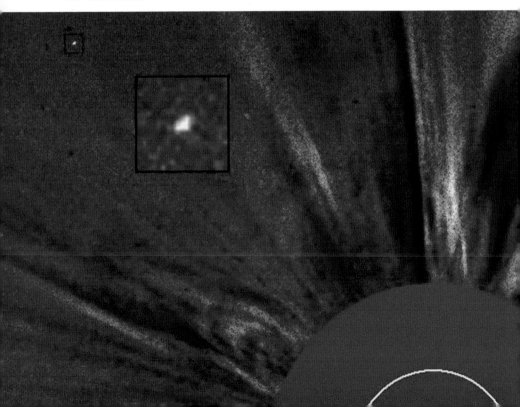

sky above earth. When many meteors burn up in the sky and make a light show above Earth, they are called meteor showers.

Comets and Meteors

Sometimes cosmic comet dust makes a halo around the sun, which can be seen as zodiacal light, a beautiful triangle of light in the sky just before or after sunset. Every day more than a hundred tons of cosmic dust—the weight of fifty elephants—fall to Earth as meteors. Meteors come in all sizes. A few meteors are huge, but most meteors are about the size of a grain of sand. Many brightly burning meteors are the size of a pea or a walnut.

Every year in August, Earth passes through the orbit of comet Swift-Tuttle, and people watch the **Perseid** meteor shower. Two meteor showers come from Halley's comet—the **Eta Aquarids** in May and the **Orionids** in October. Meteor showers are named after the constellation of stars where they appear in the sky.

The greatest meteor showers are called the **Leonids**, so named because they appear to come from the Leo constellation of stars. The Leonid meteors orbit with the comet Tempel-Tuttle and appear in mid-November.

When a huge number of meteors appears in the sky, it is called a meteor storm. Between 1994 and 2001, the Leonid showers turned to storms. Bright meteors lit up the sky, sometimes several at a time. Dr. Glenn Peterson reported seeing about seven hundred meteors per hour above Joshua Tree National Park in the California desert. Several fireballs exploded, lighting up the night sky and leaving blue-green trails that lasted for several minutes.

Even in cities, where lights and pollution usually make meteor viewing impossible, the

Hundreds of meteors from the Leonid shower light up the sky above Joshua Tree National Park in California.

light show was spectacular. Such amazing meteor storms happen when Earth is passing through a very thick region of comet dust, which may include small comets the size of a house. November is also the time when the most small comets hit the atmosphere of Earth, creating a blanket of clouds high in the sky.

Heavenly Weather

Louis Frank, a scientist at the University of Iowa, thinks that a thousand such house-sized comets strike Earth's atmosphere every hour. The small comets are nearly invisible—a million times smaller than bright comets with big tails, such as Halley's comet. They do not contain much rock dust or sodium and have no iron or other metals to make them glow brightly or create big tails.

These small comets are mostly made of frozen water, like loosely packed snowballs. They have only a very thin shell of dark carbon dust to hold them together as they travel among the stars. If they enter the atmosphere around Earth, the electrical field in the atmosphere strips away the thin layer of dark dust and the snowball usually breaks up about eight hundred miles above Earth.

By the time pieces of the comet fall to about six hundred miles above Earth, the snowball has been turned into clouds of water **vapor** by

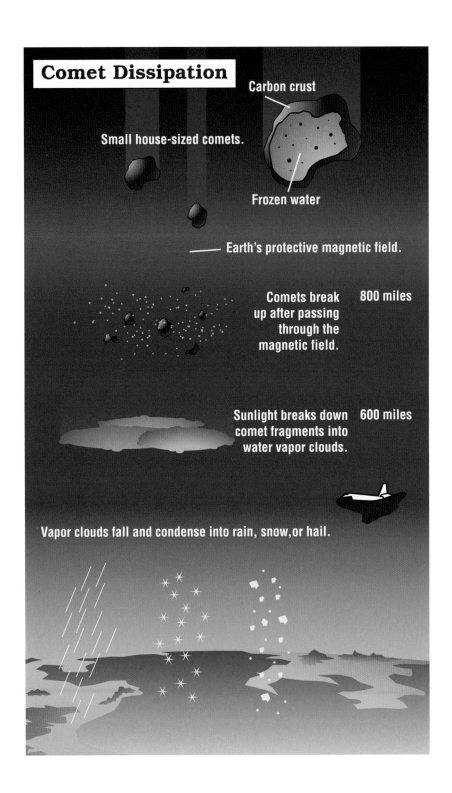

Comet Dissipation

Carbon crust

Small house-sized comets.

Frozen water

—— Earth's protective magnetic field.

Comets break up after passing through the magnetic field.   800 miles

Sunlight breaks down comet fragments into water vapor clouds.   600 miles

Vapor clouds fall and condense into rain, snow, or hail.

the rays of the sun. The water then falls from the clouds as gentle cosmic rain. Sometimes it also falls as snow or even as large ice balls known as hail. The incoming water from small comets may be responsible for all the water in the oceans and in our atmosphere. Comets may also be the seeds that help create the clouds that protect and veil Earth from the burning sun and the freezing cold of outer space.

Seeds of Life

Comets are born when solar systems are created, and thousands of comets over thousands of years may have carried the seeds of life to Earth. They contain the basic elements that make life on Earth possible, such as carbon—which is basic to life-forms—water for clouds and rain, and gases to make the air we breathe and atmosphere around us. They also contain amino acids, the building blocks of life. With their ability to travel through the universe, comets appear in many forms, from cosmic stardust to gentle rain.

4

Mysteries of the Comet

When comets fall to Earth, they are usually torn apart by the electrical storms in the upper atmosphere, turning into ice crystals and clouds about fifty miles or more above Earth. Any pieces that survive may enter the warmer layers of atmosphere closer to Earth as meteors. Most meteors then burn up in the warm atmosphere, but sometimes pieces survive this layer of protection, too. If a piece of comet survives to fall to Earth, it is called a meteorite.

Billions of years ago while the solar system was forming, scientists believe Earth was bombarded by large comets and other kinds of giant meteorites, making craters and impact basins all over the planet. An impact basin is a huge crater caused by a sudden impact, or collision, of a giant meteorite crashing into the planet. Scientists believe at least one more giant meteor hit Earth 65 million years ago, when the dinosaurs became extinct. Scientist Luis Alvarez, who led the way to proving this theory, believes the meteorite was a truly giant comet.

Death of the Dinosaurs

In 1980 Luis Alvarez and his coworkers set out to prove the theory that a large meteorite caused the extinction of the dinosaurs. Many scientists joined the search, and in 1990 they found a huge impact basin more than a hundred miles wide under the town of Chicxulub (CHEEK-shoo-loob) in the northern Yucatán peninsula in Mexico.

Artwork depicts the giant Chicxulub meteor approaching Earth. Scientists believe the meteor caused the extinction of dinosaurs.

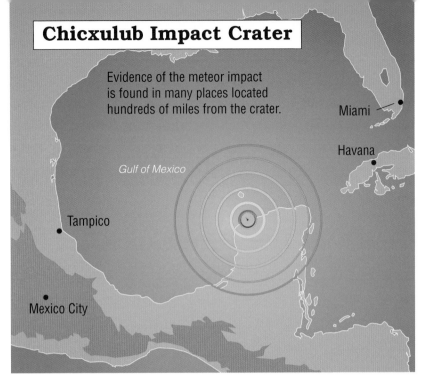

Chicxulub Impact Crater

Evidence of the meteor impact is found in many places located hundreds of miles from the crater.

Miami

Havana

Gulf of Mexico

Tampico

Mexico City

One hundred eighty miles from Chicxulub, scientists found another ring of the old giant impact basin. The true size was hard to measure, since the whole basin is buried under a mile of limestone, like the ocean floor nearby. Close to the impact basin, scientists found glassy beads called tektites that formed when melted liquid rock from the basin was hurled into the sky. As the liquid rocks flew through the air, they were shaped into teardrops, flattened balls, and dumbbells.

They also found shocked quartz, grains of sand that were hit so suddenly and so hard, it changed the structure of the atoms in the sand. Scientists think the fireball was so big, it set all the forests of the world on fire and killed all the dinosaurs—along with most other creatures on land and in the sea. Shocked quartz may have been blown so high, it went into orbit and came down all over Earth! A veil of dust and ash covered the sun, creating a long, dark winter. Most of the plants died in the sea and on land, and most of the animals on the planet died of starvation.

The whole world was covered with soot from the burning forests, as well as elements that rained down from the meteorite itself. These include a hard whitish-yellow metal called iridium, a hard bluish-white metal called osmium, and right-handed amino acids, the building blocks for unknown life-forms from outer space.

When the sun came back out and life began to rebuild, new life-forms may have begun to form from the amino acids that rained down into the sea. These amino acids are often found in comets and are part of the reason why scientists believe it was a comet that ended the age of the dinosaurs and began the age of mammals.

Monahans Fall

While giant comets very rarely fall to Earth, smaller pieces of comets, called meteorites, often fall to the ground, causing little damage. On March 22, 1998, one such meteorite fell close to seven children playing basketball in Monahans, Texas. It was a piece of comet with its crust burned off by Earth's atmosphere. It

The skull of a triceratops lies among the burnt trees and ashes left from the devastating collision of the Chicxulub meteor with Earth.

looked like a glowing white soccer ball and was still warm when it landed. (Such meteorites are said to freeze over soon after they fall. If one is found, putting it in a freezer preserves it.)

The children sold a large piece of the comet for $23,000, while a smaller piece was sent to the laboratories of NASA's Johnson Space Center in Houston. There, scientists carefully opened the little piece of comet and found tiny bubbles of water trapped in purple and blue crystals of nearly pure rock salt. This is the same thing as ordinary table salt or the salt in the oceans.

The water that the astronomers found was the same water that flowed through the comet when it was formed at the beginning of the solar system. This means that the water in the crystals could be 4.5 billion years old—older than Earth! The salt in the water had turned purple and blue while traveling through space.

Yukon Fall

Two years later, on the morning of January 18, 2000, a comet the size of a school bus fell in the Yukon Territory in Canada. In the morning light, a long shooting star of many colors blazed through the sky for about fifteen seconds. As the comet broke up into pieces, two sonic booms were heard all the way from Alaska through northwestern Canada.

Two flares lit up the sky, and witnesses said that the brighter one glowed with a blue-green light ten times as bright as daylight. Witnesses heard sizzling sounds and smelled a terrible odor, like sulfur or burning hot metal and rock. The comet's dust tail hung in the air for a few hours, pushed along and sculpted by the winds high in the sky.

A comet the size of a school bus crashes in the Yukon Territory in Canada, sending a flash of colors through the sky.

Most of the comet broke apart and burned up in the atmosphere before landing. But hundreds of very rare, very fragile space rocks shattered on the ice or landed in the soft snow. The largest pieces were about the size of a charcoal briquette.

The meteorites were dust balls that had bubbled off the surface of a comet passing close to the sun. They contained many odd ingredients, such as tiny nanodiamonds and strong-smelling organic compounds. (Nanodiamonds are tiny little diamonds that are formed from the pressure of two carbon-type comets or asteroids colliding.) The smelly organic compounds include some of the chemicals that are basic to life on Earth.

Mysterious Comets

Many scientists are fascinated by the interesting things they find in comets that fall to Earth. In 1997 scientists studying the Hale-Bopp comet found some chemicals similar to those they think led to life on Earth. The hot sun changes some of these chemicals into a misty cloud that contains some of the most common simple gases on Earth—carbon, hydrogen, nitrogen, and oxygen.

Comets also carry water and other life-giving elements from the far reaches of outer space to the warm regions around the sun. Some scientists think that comets may have flown in all the elements necessary to sustain life on Earth. Over thousands of years, comets may have flown enough water into Earth's atmosphere to fill up all the oceans.

Comets are mysterious and beautiful baby planets. Scientists continue to study the many wonderful life-forms they bring from far away. In comets that have fallen to Earth, they have found a jellylike space goo that contains all the amino acids that make life on Earth. From the rain and clouds to life itself, the mysterious comets billions of years old may have played a major role in creating the world as it is today.

Glossary

atmosphere: The envelope of gas held around Earth by gravity.

gas: Not in the form of solid or liquid; in the form of a misty cloud.

gravity: The natural force of attraction that pulls objects toward a heavenly body, such as the sun or Earth pulling on a comet.

ion: Particle having an electric charge.

nucleus: The central basic part around which the other parts gather.

orbit: The path of a heavenly body around another body.

particle: A very small part, the tiniest speck.

reflect: To throw back light from a surface.

solar wind: The flow of high-speed ionized particles from the sun's surface into outer space.

vapor: Barely visible misty clouds hanging in the air.

When to See Meteor Showers

Quadrantids: January 1–6 before dawn; about sixty per hour; blue meteors with fine tails.

Eta Aquarids: April 24–May 20, just before dawn; thirty-five per hour; low in sky; associated with comet Halley.

Capricornids: July–August, after midnight; five per hour; bright meteors.

Alpha Capricornids: July 15–August 25, all night; five per hour; yellow, slow fireballs.

Perseids: July 23–August 20, best before dawn; eighty per hour; many bright, fast meteors with tails; associated with comet Swift-Tuttle 1737, 1862, 1992.

Orionids: October 16–27, after midnight; twenty-five per hour; fast with fine tails; associated with comet Halley.

Taurids: October 20–November 30, all night; ten per hour; very slow meteors; associated with the parent body of comet Enke.

Leonids: November 15–20, after midnight; ten per hour; fast, bright meteors with fine tails; associated with comet Tempel-Tuttle.

Geminids: December 7–16, after midnight; one hundred per hour; many bright meteors; few tails; associated with asteroid Phaeton.

For Further Exploration

Isaac Asimov, *Comets and Meteors*. Milwaukee: Gareth Stevens Publishing, 1990. Discusses the mysteries connected with famous comets and meteors.

Franklyn M. Branley, *What Happened to the Dinosaurs?* New York: Harper and Row, 1989. Describes the theory that comets caused the extinction of the dinosaurs.

E.C. Krupp, *The Comet and You.* New York: Macmillan, 1989. Describes Halley's comet and compares it with other comets.

Seymour Simon, *Comets, Meteors, and Asteroids.* New York: Morrow Junior Books, 1994. Explains how comets can cause meteor showers, how an asteroid may have caused the extinction of the dinosaurs, and what meteorites tell scientists about other space objects.

Paul P. Sipiera, *Comets and Meteor Showers.* Chicago: Childrens Press, 1997. Tells where comets come from and how they travel and describes their relationship to meteor showers.

Index

Picture Credits

Cover and Title Page Photo: © Richard Cummins/CORBIS (main); Tony and Daphne Hallas/Science Source/Photo Researchers (inset)

© AFP/CORBIS, 11 (inset), 26

Art Archive/Royal Society/Eileen Tweedy, 8

Associated Press, AP, 11 (main), 20

© Julian Baum/Science Source/Photo Researchers, 24

© Richard Cummins/CORBIS, 28

© Tony and Daphne Hallas/Science Source/Photo Researchers, 19

© David A. Hardy/Science Source/Photo Researchers, 5

Chris Jouan, 6, 16, 23, 30, 34

© Claus Luneau/Foci/Bonnier, Publications/Science Source/Photo Researchers, 15

© Pekka Parvianen/Science Source/Photo Researchers, 38

© Roger Ressmeyer/CORBIS, 9

© D. Van Ravenswaay/Science Source/Photo Researchers, 33, 36

About the Authors

P.M. Boekhoff is an author of more than a dozen nonfiction books for young readers and has illustrated many book covers. In addition, Ms. Boekhoff creates theatrical scenic works and other large paintings. In her spare time, she writes poetry and fiction, studies herbal medicine, and tends her garden.

Stuart A. Kallen is the author of more than 150 nonfiction books for children and young adults. He has written extensively about Native Americans and American history. In addition, Mr. Kallen has written award-winning children's videos and television scripts. In his spare time, he is a singer/songwriter/guitarist in San Diego, California.